The Great Rabourn Family Missionary Adventure

Brian L. Rabourn

Munich, Germany

2001

FOREWARD

The Great Rabourn Family Missionary Adventure

Brian L. Rabourn

Grand Rapids, Michigan, USA

2019

A title such as *The Great Rabourn Family Missionary Adventure* is obviously grandiose. It is intended to be reminiscent of the movie, *The Great Race*, an old Blake Edwards film with Tony Curtis and Natalie Wood which spoofs the overdramatic but loveable characteristics of the silent film days.

The book tells a story, but it is not a continuous narrative, nor is it finished. It is not a novel, because everything in it is fact. It is not the history of a church or a ministry. It is my testimony, on behalf of Dorothy and I, about how we came to give away almost everything we owned to move our young family of five to Slovenia in 1997. As a personal testimony, it is far from a ministry guide or theological meditation. Rather, it is a patchwork of observations on how we heard from God, and what we did about it. It is our wish that the Holy Spirit will use this testimony to encourage someone who perceives a calling from God, but is uncertain what to do. Although I not able to mentor prospective ministers or missionaries, I can write about our own experiences in the faithful expectation that God will use the story for his purposes. My responsibility is to testify to what I have experienced: "As for us, we cannot help speaking about what we have seen and heard" (Acts 4:20, New International Version).

A significant amount of time has passed since I wrote the story, and I like to think I learned to write properly in the eighteen years since, especially considering my subsequent education. Except for reworking some of the grammar and paragraphing, however, I have not revised the content. I wrote it straight through in two days in Munich, compelled as I was in my spirit to explain what we did over the four years previous. When it was done, I was certain that God wanted me to leave it without revision, so that the reality of our confusion and struggles in trying to follow God would not be exchanged for balanced syntax. Sometime soon, I will add at least two more parts. One, there is the story of what happened as a result of the dot-com bubble and the attacks on the World Trade Center, that slowly increased pressure on us until we were eventually compelled to leave Europe in December of 2003. Two, there is the version of my story as told by my wife, Dorothy, which will invariably include what we have been doing in Europe of late.

Publishing this story fulfills a personal vow I made a very long time ago. This means I will not keep any money that I receive from making my testimony public, neither from eBook sales, nor from gifts designated "Rabourn Family Adventure." Any such money will be sent to one of the churches where we were members in Ljubljana or Munich, or one of the ministers we worked for in Europe, or the Teen Challenge rehab in Koper, Slovenia. Feel free to contact my wife at rabourncrew@yahoo.com

In late May 1997, on a warm summer afternoon, Dorothy was lying on our bed with a sore throat and a bit of a fever. She probably had strep throat again. She had been sleeping all day, on-again, off-again, but when I entered the room she was awake.

"You have to get up now, dear," I said.

"Why?" she replied, "I'm sick."

I said, "Well...ah...you have to get up because I just sold the bed to a family outside."

She didn't say anything more; she just groaned as she dragged herself out of the bedroom.

"Honey," I said.

"Yeah," she grunted.

"Leave the blanket; I sold that, too."

After Dorothy sat down in the kid's bedroom, I returned to the back yard where virtually everything we owned was spread all over, in only the barest semblance of order. A couple of strangers were there, looking things over, trying to decide if there was anything worth buying. Here and there, people bought things for a few dollars; the weight lifting set Dorothy gave me for my birthday, the fish tank I got for her, children's books which represented hundreds of hours Dorothy had spent reading to our kids. The fact is that almost every physical object, which stood for something nostalgic, was there, and it all had to go. I didn't know at that point exactly how many days we had left, but the deal was made with my brother and people were already waiting for us.

The plan was that I would call the airlines every day to find the cheapest possible one-way flight to Ljubljana, Slovenia. Once we were gone, my brother Dan would fix-up our house and sell it for us. To save money, we would not pay for the shipment of any possessions. Rather, we would take only those things that fit into the two check-in bags per ticket allowed by the airlines. A few things were to be stored with friends, but with the exception of the most personal items, everything was to be liquidated. Why were we going? How long would we be there? What school would our children attend? How would we earn income? What good could we possibly do, seeing that I wasn't a certified minister?

I had a thousand such questions on hold. I didn't have all the answers I wanted, but there was no doubt in my mind that the hand of God was directing us. He was not only sending us to a foreign land to witness about Jesus Christ but He also miraculously promised to sustain us in the places He would send us. Knowing this, I knew what had to be done. I hardened my heart against emotion and got rid of nearly everything we had accumulated over ten years of marriage with three children.

The first inkling I had that I might be called into mission work came when I was very young, around seven or eight years old. Mel and Deanna Ferguson, Baptist missionaries to Bolivia, came to my church to talk about their ministry. I felt very strongly at that time there could be absolutely no way I would ever be even remotely interested in anything like what they were talking about. In fact, for the next twenty-five years or so I would be strongly repulsed by anything to do with missionaries, even skipping church when Corrie Ten Boom came to speak. At that time, I didn't know it, but a spiritual battle had begun over my future.

In those early years of my life and Christianity I had no interest in Paul and his missionary journeys. I was fascinated by the Old Testament Bible stories. My brothers and I often took turns using mom's flannel-graph to teach each other stories about Moses, Joseph, Elijah, and many others. Stories about Jesus were special, to me belonging neither to the Old Testament or the New Testament. The entire Bible from Genesis through the crucifixion of Jesus was interesting, but after that there was a problem. When it came to Paul and his missionary journeys, I felt an aversion to everything associated with them. I can still recall the feeling it was so distinct.

In high school, I took all of the math and science classes possible. Otherwise, I had a wide range of interests, limited only by time. In a perfect world, I would have taken all of the courses offered. All but one, that is, and that one was foreign languages. At the time, I could not see that the strong aversion I had for languages closely matched my negative feelings about missionaries. Of course, in hindsight, it is obvious that I could have made things a lot easier by facing my calling, but I was so completely sure I would never have anything to do with languages or cultures, I ignored all opportunities for related education and experience, including the long-standing offer from my uncle to visit my two cousins who lived in Berlin, Germany.

I think it was in mid-year 1985 when Mark Buntain came to my church, which was then First Assembly of God, Grand

9

Rapids, Michigan. He was a well-known missionary pastor in Calcutta, India. This man was really something. He moved me so much that day I knew that I would never be the same. I don't remember anything specific about his message other than the fact that even though he ministered in a very negative and difficult place, he couldn't wait to get back. He was so urgent about it I felt embarrassed just watching him. He literally trembled all over when he talked about getting back to India. I thought he'd hyperventilate at any point while he spoke. It seemed he wasn't interested too much about the attention he was getting from his pastoral hosts and the church. He was so passionate about "his people," he apparently didn't think about anything else. I had never in my life seen a man so totally committed to anything or anyone, and it was disturbing.

At the end of the service, he gave a kind of altar call I was not used to. He didn't push the congregation so much as plead with us to give ourselves to "whatever" God would ask, "whenever" He asked, and to go "wherever" He would send us. I knew God was speaking to me. It wasn't like talking about a career and the corresponding salary or thinking about the military or what my dad thought I should do. For the first time I can remember, I had a desire to put myself in God's hands without reservation or condition. I wanted it all, whatever that might be.

As two or three thousand people got out of the pews to kneel in the aisles and pray, I knelt, too. As Mark Buntain walked among the people, praying here and there, I became increasingly agitated. I focused intently and felt the move of God profoundly. I worked myself into a certainty that God was about to choose me for some grand work.

From the time I was in elementary school, I secretly thought I would grow up to become a great man of God. As I focused on the Old Testament stories, I always pictured some larger than life miracle I would perform, just like Elijah of old, such as commanding rain to cease from the lawn of the White House.

I was at a unique time in my life when I had zero debt, no commitments, no girlfriend; I didn't even have a job. I thought it was a fine opportunity for God to choose me and use me. I believed that this great veteran missionary pastor was about to put his hand on me and call me out to return with him to India. I already had it all decided; I would accept and be off on an adventure within days. Who was I to say "NO" if God wanted me to become the worthy successor to this famous man? I was ready, or so I thought.

As he began coming my way in the midst of so many people, I all but jumped up for excitement. Closer and closer he stepped around the people praying until his shoe stopped right next to me. This was it. In a moment, I would be chosen. Then, his shoe moved on. He kept going, moving between people and praying as before, but he neither touched me nor spoke. I was crushed. By the time he returned to the front of the sanctuary I had all but melted into the carpet for disappointment. I was apparently not the worthy successor to a great man, after all.

In spite of my foolishness and pride, God did not completely let me down. I think it was the very next week that Pastor Benson started a new series entitled, "Stay Home," in which he preached about practical witnessing and becoming more a part of the local church and helping ministry that was already in place. There was much to be said about waiting for God's timing. I was encouraged and got involved with teaching Sunday School. During the following year I married Dorothy and started a family. I didn't have any thoughts about moving to a place like Slovenia. I am sure that I didn't know where Slovenia was. I'd heard of Yugoslavia, of course, but I didn't have any mental images.

Although I didn't even know where or what Slovenia was, I thought enough of my commitment to go wherever God would send me that before Dorothy and I got married, I warned her that I "might be called into foreign missions," so she should seriously consider it before marrying me. In fact, I insisted that she agree to go to Calcutta, India with me if God should call me there. When she took a full two weeks to think about it before she even gave her answer, I knew that this young woman took giving her word very seriously.

At that time, if the tables were turned and she had asked me to consider "whatever" missionary calling she might have, I suppose I would have given a hasty "yes" because it would have been the spiritual thing to say. It irked me that she would not give herself to me one hundred percent, as she insisted that God would surely tell both of us if and when He actually called us to something so risky. Ever since that time, however, I have increasingly found myself to be hesitant to take any significant action if Dorothy does not confirm my choices and direction.

Sometime around the beginning of the nineties, (as I recall, the Assembly of God "Decade of Harvest"), there was an especially good missions conference at our church. While in corporate worship, where I often hear strong direction from God, I "saw" Germany in my mind and believed that God was telling me to go to Germany. I saw an outdoor assembly of people who were before a covered platform. The people had one arm raised in Nazi salute. In a moment, I was looking at the same physical place, also with a crowd, but this time everyone had both arms raised in worship to Jesus. I felt God tell me to go "to the place where the Nazis were." At that moment, I didn't know which city the vision was referring to. When I told Dorothy about the vision, she matter-of-factly said that she saw something similar.

Later, we came to understand that Munich was the target city and we eventually stood in the exact place I saw in my vision six or seven years earlier. The place in the vision was the Feldherrnhalle, situated on the southern side of Odeonsplatz, the very place where the German army stopped Hitler's famous attempt to forcibly take over the government in 1922. Some of the beer halls, which were the scene of some passionate early speeches contributing to the formation of the Nazi Party remain today in a reconstructed form within a five-minute walk of this busy city square.

If I could, I would not mention this vision at all, because several of my German friends will read it. One depressing thing I have learned since coming to Germany is that the people here carry a burden because the world will not let the Germans forget WWII. I don't feel equal to judging this attitude, but I can see damage in the lives of some of the sons and grandsons of the wartime population. It is important, however, to relate how God spoke regarding our mission calling for two reasons.

First of all, He used it to move us to Munich when the time came. If our mission destination were not clear, we never would have left our home on the outskirts of Ljubljana. Secondly, God connected the vision with the wartime to begin opening my eyes to the spiritual condition in Germany. I do not mean that I find a need to combat spiritual forces of Nazism here. Sure, there are some extremists here, but there are probably as many in any modern culture, including the United States. What I find here is a generation restless for an identity free from a stigma they did not create. There are clear spiritual bondages, and some are related to what happened before, but in gardening terms, it's more an absence of fruit than the presence of weeds.

When Dorothy told me she saw a similar vision to mine in the missions convention, I was skeptical at first. I know it indicates a lack of assurance on my part in God's vision, but the fact is that I wasn't sure that I hadn't imagined it. I certainly did not see a vision that was clear as a film, or beyond all doubting, like some I have read about. What increased my doubts was the knowledge that I had always had some mental connection with Germany, either because of my uncle, who was stationed in Berlin for many years, or the many WWII movies I watched as a kid. Perhaps it was just natural that when thinking of a foreign country I would think of Germany. I was also a little worried because I doubted that there was a real missionary need; surely the German church was the same as in the United States.

I should probably have dived right in and started a serious study of the German language. We didn't know it, but a solid five years were to elapse before any confirming event took place. During that time we sometimes talked about Germany and took note of silly things, like the usher who we thought could speak German because of his old-world accent, but we were never able to bring our vision into the practical world. We were too busy with the cares of working and raising a family. I suppose we expected God to do everything. The fact is that He was not going to do everything, but neither did He leave us to wonder about it indefinitely.

By the time God moved again, we were sick of talking big about how we had a "calling" to Germany. We had tried on various attitudes, mostly related to our lofty views about some "great work." I don't think our friends were very impressed. During this same time, I felt more and more that I was a prisoner of my work as a quality manager in the automobile parts industry. Increasingly, the things I said in church or in connection with spirituality were like a fantasy when compared to how I felt my life was based on my work. By late 1993, work had begun to consume about sixty hours a week, sometimes a little more.

After a while, I began to dislike my work. In the beginning, I was very proud to be working with engineers and big companies. I did a good job at Bil-Mac, a small but solid machining company in Grandville, MI. I foolishly threw away my manager position in this company where good work was both appreciated and rewarded. I gave it up for a more subordinate position, (with a 35% increase in salary), in an arm of a huge company where I was sure I would rise to a much higher position through my hard work and superior skills. I soon found out that my skills and hard work weren't even noticed by the officials of this monster of a company. It was filled with problems, politics, and dishonesty. This was not a provincial company; it was a finger on the hand of the arm of one of the top twenty largest corporations in America at the time. The pressure became nearly unbearable, as I found all too late that I preferred a smaller, family-owned company.

As the months wore on, and I learned to hate my job truly and everything related to it, I slowly realized that I was in danger of trading a calling from God for something that I thought I wanted because it made me feel important and paid very well. Little did I know how ugly it could get. In two years, we went through three quality managers, two plant managers, and almost a dozen other staff changes. By the time the purchasing manager up and walked out one day never to return with no notice whatsoever, it just seemed typical of the environment. I wanted out. I prayed that I could now jump out of my work and into that calling from God I had neglected.

I was not a good fit for any local ministry beyond the Sunday school I worked in. I therefore had quite a way to go before I could escape the bondage of that career I thought I wanted, but the direction was uncertain. I wanted a quick escape from my situation, but God wanted to bring me through a set of experiences to teach me in a hands-on way that I would never forget. Spiritually, I felt as if I were regressing, rather than progressing, throwing around tired religious remarks and resenting my wife's efforts to give direction. God wanted to bring me along all the same. It's just that He wanted to bring me to a place I had never been before.

In the first half of 1995, God began to move aggressively in our lives so that we would be permanently changed. There was some kind of anointing service at First Assembly where the pastors and elders formed a "tunnel," and the entire church passed through single file, each receiving an oil anointing and many prayers. Just before we reached the front of the church, I bent over and told my three kids to pray about Germany when they were prayed for. As soon as we cleared the "tunnel," Amanda knelt on the floor; many others were there praying too, so I joined them and prayed. When I got up, I saw that Amanda was still praying. After waiting a while, I told her to come with me, and we returned to our pew. A little while later, I noticed that she was on the floor at the pew, praying.

I was amazed because this was not like her. She was very energetic for the age of eight, and here she was exhibiting more earnest focus than would be usual for adults in such a service. I leaned down and asked her if she would like to go back to the "altar" (the front of the church) to pray. For the next hour and a half she was somewhere else. For a while she would lay right down on her face, completely motionless. Then, she would rise to her knees and lift her hands for a while before returning to a prostrate position, all without opening her eyes or showing any sign that she knew she was with me in church. She did not speak at all. She kept on, even when the rest of the church moved from prayer into rather loud praise. With more than three thousand people standing and praising, Amanda did not come out of her trance for a single moment.

Later, when we were the very last people there, she became aware of me and got up. I sent Dorothy and the kids out to pick up a couple of pizzas, so I could find out what happened without any distractions. I sat down with Amanda and asked her what she saw. I said absolutely nothing else so that there would be no taint from me in what she replied.

Amanda explained how she saw Jesus appear to her in a form "just like in the Sunday school books." He picked her up and held her a while. He talked to her. He told her she was special and that He loved her very much. She saw the gates of heaven and many very large "mansions with yellow streets." Jesus told her that the reason He had not yet come back was that he wanted "a big feast." He also showed her "a dark place where people who don´t believe in Jesus go," and she cried. He also showed her "how the sky looks when Jesus comes, with lasers shining out of the clouds and every color of the rainbow before He comes shooting out of the clouds." She said she felt like she wanted to tell everyone in the world about what she saw.

Regarding Germany, she also said that we "would go to Pennsylvania and Germany." It was incredible, and I was overwhelmed. Here was what I had thought was unthinkable: an undeniable move of God. There was simply no way I could make claims of emotionalism, imagination, or hallucination. It was more encouraging to hear these things from my eight-year-old than if I had seen the vision myself. She was so innocent minded there was no denying any of it. I felt changed, sure that everything we were praying about would quickly come together. In subsequent weeks, there was more encouragement. When the children's pastor asked for Spirit-filled kids to pray for each other, Amanda prayed for many of the kids. So many kids were filled with the Spirit and "fell out" all around on the floor in the Spirit that one of the teachers called for more kids to come over because "Amanda has the anointing!"

The job I took that year was to be my escape from the negative, gut-wrenching grind of the automobile industry. It was to be the place in my life from which I would get serious with God and move ahead. God, however, was not ready to be directed by me. It was He who did the directing. Earlier, I had ignored the call of God to follow a career in production and engineering. Now that I had reached my limit, in my estimation, I wanted out. God was not ready to release me from trial. The "escape job" was from God, all right. It was to be a lesson for me in how quickly I could get sucked back into a wrong focus and spiritual mediocrity. The working conditions became worse than ever, and my previous job seemed good by comparison. My hours reached an all-time high of seventy-five to eighty-five hours per week. I only lasted through the summer and fall to Thanksgiving before I couldn`t stomach the demands and the politics, and I quit.

The year 1996, from beginning to end, was the most extraordinary year imaginable as far as work was concerned. I tried to control what was left of my career so that I would finally be free to prepare for God's work. Three different times I called on God to meet specific job conditions that I would state, and three times He would answer, giving me precisely what I had asked for. Three times that year, I had to learn that there is no such thing as "making room for God." I had to learn that I must obey God in a straightforward way, or not. There could be no "working it out," as I called my vacillating and doubt. To do His will, which I had taken the initiative to ask for, I would have to move my life out of the way.

With the first job that year, I thought that I needed a new company that didn't have a quality system. Then, I could relax, do what I did before at Bil-Mac, building up the system bit by bit, spending the rest of my time on God's plan for the missions. But I had forgotten how difficult it could be to sell the managers on the kinds of procedures that are essential in the long run, though negative in the short term during implementation. It had taken fully four years to install a complete program at Bil-Mac, and I didn't intend to stay in the long run.

Next, I thought that I needed an established company with an existing system needing simple fine-tuning. Then, I could relax, make some improvements, spending the rest of my time on God's plan for the missions. But I should have known that it is even harder to revise a system that works reasonably well than it would have been to install a completely new one. There are many "battles" to be fought with managers who think that existing procedures are good enough. MacDonald's Industrial Products had been in operation for decades before I was out of school. I couldn't change everything in a few months.

Finally, I thought that what I needed was an established company, run by excellent people with morals, who would surely appreciate me and allow me to be the fully qualified and mature quality manager I was. This time, I was really without excuse. I was hired into Double "J" Molding at an excellent wage, my highest ever. The owner of the company was a Christian, and so was the engineering manager. While I was in for my interview, I saw the painting behind the owner's desk of a businessman listening to Jesus lecture him on how to run his business. When I asked about the picture, the owner told me all about how he started the company in a pole barn with just one machine, years ago. The company had grown to the point that it was finally undergoing the audit, which would lead to the achievement of the QS9000 quality certification. It was an excellent company.

Also, the owner was quite interested in my family, church activity, and me, personally. He even told me that he felt God told him to give me the job; it was everything I could ask for and more. How was it possible that I couldn't get into it? Every day, all I could think about was "how will I get from here to Germany and God's plan for my life?" I felt like a fool; I had a wife and three kids. Surely I should wait on God's plan and concentrate on work. The missions would always be there, wouldn't it?

Every day became a tedious burden. I knew that the boss could see something was wrong with me, but I never told him about it. I never told him that from the first day, I was planning to leave when it became possible. I felt a little dishonest, but I didn't know what else I should do at that time. It seemed too hard to move toward the mission field, so I had to work. Quality was my business, so I thought I had to stay in it. Here was the best possible set-up, however, and I was failing to impress anyone, the least of all, God.

I probably owe Bill Maatman an apology for this, but I know he did not make a mistake by hiring me. I believe what he said about God telling him to hire me, but not because God wanted me to work there, but because God was in the process of destroying my ability to be satisfied with a "normal" life. Of course, I had asked for it. I had told God many times I was willing to go wherever He sent me to help anyone He showed me. This was the final turning point in my mission calling. I finally understood how the plan of God couldn't be fitted into a life; it must be the plan for that life. For guys like Bill, the owner, I'm sure that the plan for his life was to work and witness to people that come and go. God bless him in that. For me, however, the plan of God required a major change. So, as a result, I quit my job in January 1997 without another plan. I firmly believed that God was directing me, and to stay would be to allow money to take over as the guiding force in my life. It wasn't easy, and it was certainly no joke. I had a wife and three children; I knew I couldn't expect anyone outside of Dorothy and our kids to understand or approve, and that's the truth.

There was only one thing left to do: fast and pray. For about a month, eating soup and bread, I called upon God to show me what to do. I quickly received a strong impression that I needed to contact Steve Telzerow, the missionary to Slovenia that we had met that summer before during the Telzerow's itineration in the United States. That in itself was quite extraordinary.

A year or so before, a missionary by the name of MacIsaac came to our church. He was on the way to a ministry in Lithuania, but he had already ministered in Germany for a time. Although I don't recall how we met, when he learned that we were interested in going into the mission field, he was kind enough to take time and come to our home to pray for us. He prayed that God would set up "divine appointments" in our life, which would move us along in His will.

Within a couple of months of meeting the MacIsaacs, after Dorothy spoke in a ladies group in our church about our desire to reach people in Europe, Barbara Telzerow, who we had never met before, approached her and said, flat out, "you're going to Germany." She invited us to visit to talk and pray, especially since her husband Steve had been a campus minister in Germany for about five years before his transfer to the country Slovenia. It was funny because the Telzerows were the missionary family that my Sunday school class was assigned to learn about and pray for that very year. During that visit with the Telzerows, Steve and Barbara talked with us, prayed with us, and agreed that we could visit them in Slovenia sometime.

Now it was the following January, and I needed to contact Steve and Barbara. I had a regular address and an e-mail address, but neither was needed. Although their itineration was complete and they had been back in Slovenia for six months or so, not due to return for three more years, they unexpectedly showed up again in our church (where Steve originated). They came right in the middle of my fasting and prayer time; we were very encouraged. Steve was not in any hurry to tell me what to do, but he was very supportive and kept a passive welcome open if I wanted to visit them in Slovenia. If I were looking for someone to help push me into an overseas move, it wasn't going to be him, but neither was he going to be someone to tell me that God wasn't speaking to me or that I must be wrong.

Somewhat in connection with the great revival that was taking place in Brownsville, Florida, our church was also experiencing a revival. The revival had certain aspects of it that matched the established prophecy concerning the future of our church, namely, that it would be a "lighthouse" ministry that would give out in every direction, sometimes over great distances. During the revival, many people were compelled to go, officially as well as unofficially, to various cities and churches specifically to anoint with oil and pray for the revival of the church and the move of the Holy Spirit

That same winter, just days or weeks after we saw the Telzerows unexpectedly, the Brownsville church, which was in revival sent a ministry team to our church with all the principle leaders, preacher, and evangelist that had been ministering to hundreds of thousands for the last couple of years. Knowing in her heart that we needed to be near what was happening, Dorothy sneaked us into the area-wide, pastors-only meeting by volunteering us for nursery back up. When we weren't needed by the nursery any longer, we were allowed to sit in the back of the meeting. When Pastor Kilpatrick called for everyone to pass in a note with an "impossible request" for God, "something only He can fulfill." I wrote, "Get us into Europe." Dorothy wrote, "Give me a double portion of Elisha's spirit."

During a combined Brownsville-First Assembly service in which over 8,000 people attended, filling every available corner in the church, many miraculous things happened. The Spirit of God was mighty that evening. There was a massive traffic jam. Cars were parked literally for miles in every direction, as it snowed the better part of a foot that night. Someone in the church ordered pizza from the little shop down the road we often went for pizza. Larry, the pizza delivery guy told us later what happened to him:

He said that he was driving up the road in the direction of the church when he felt something coming from the church. He didn't know what it was, but he felt so good, so happy, that he rolled down his window and put his arm out to get more and honked on the horn a few times. Later, within about a month Larry accepted Jesus into his life.

The move of God's Spirit inside the sanctuary was more than merely noticeable. It was overpowering spiritually, emotionally, and also physically. During this service, while kneeling and praying, I urgently called upon God to do something with my life. I remember telling God nothing was too much to ask; I would be willing to trade my house if need be to do His will if only He would tell me what He planned for me to do, or even what I would be allowed to do in His name. I wanted God to move in my life like He was moving in the lives of those people who had come from Florida to turn our lives upside-down.

In response to my prayers, God moved my heart with an answer. I know that He said two things to me. One, He told me "you already know everything you need to know to get into missions," and that "you are the only thing keeping you out of the mission field." This meant that God was telling me that the only reason I wasn't being used was that I wasn't doing anything. I can honestly say that I not only didn't like such a word from God, and I became a bit angry. I had wanted God to reveal something more in the way of direction, specifically with whom I would work, and how I was to get there. I felt as though I was being teased. I didn't know how to get going; someone would have to do it for me.

In the next month or so, I was forced to act. It seems strange now that the only thing lacking at times in my life was decisive action. To tell the whole truth, the reason that I don't always take decisive action is plain and simple fear, fear of being wrong, fear of failure, fear of criticism, etc. I was now faced with a sort of unofficial deadline. In a short period of time, I would be entirely without money, so if I didn't do something now, there was no telling how long it would be before God would call me out again, if ever. No, I couldn't turn back around, better that I would have stayed at the plastic molding company with the Christian boss in the first place, rather than try to go back and be sorry for the rest of my life.

But all that was in the past; I had already set myself up by dumping my career in quality and manufacturing.

During this period, our church still in revival, hundreds of people accepting Jesus and being baptized, thousands being freed to express vigorous worship together, families being reunited, husbands returning home, people getting off drugs, and more, we often went forward with the masses of people to be prayed for. Repeatedly, God moved on the elder or pastor praying to say the same thing others had told us in the Spirit, and that was that Jesus wanted us to know "I will sustain you..." No less than six times, different ministers prophetically said the same thing. There were other prophecies, but in the end, it was a repeating message until Dave Stults started laughing while praying and said "haven't I already told you, I will sustain you." That was it; we didn't receive another message.

It kept coming back to me, "I would even trade my house..." I knew what I had to do. I would sell our car to finance a trip to Slovenia to figure things out, such as where I would work (hopefully in the automobile industry) then I would sell our house to finance moving our family to Slovenia. I knew our calling was to Germany, but I had no option on Germany at the moment, so I trusted that God intended to send us to Germany by way of Slovenia, but more particularly, to Steve and Barbara Telzerow´s church

I started teaching English as a result of Steve noticing an advertisement in the American Embassy in Ljubljana. As I said before, I initially expected to work in the automobile industry in Germany, presumably in quality control. Back in 1994, when I was at United Technologies Automotive, I all but came out of my chair when I found out that UTA had a steering wheel factory in Dachau. I didn´t know where this infamous city was precisely situated, but somehow I felt I was to go there. Since coming to Germany, I have found that the requirements for engineering department work are different from what I expected, and we haven't seen a way to get in. I must admit, though, that Dorothy sincerely rejects the idea of me getting back into the auto industry in any way, shape, or form. We have grown so much more together since I escaped that life, we would rather live off a fraction of that income we once had, but be together more and with more meaning than go back to that which we consider a curse of sorts. We got our wish.

It still seems likely that the best way to finance our mission work is to teach English. I have been hesitant up to now to ask anyone for financial support because we are here to find small churches, pastors and missionaries, who need encouragement. I am not a certified minister, nor have I been sent to be a representative of any church. I don't blame my church for not showing an interest in my calling. There are normal channels for people to follow to get into full-time ministry, and I didn't have time for them in the past. Now, however, God is leading us into a work that I think people will have a hard time criticizing. That is, we are here to work and use what we have to help and encourage wherever it is needed, wherever God indicates.

Back to our point of departure, I found that by selling our only car, I was able to get enough money to visit Slovenia. It was tight, though. We have some friends who believed in our calling without whom we could not have done anything. First of all, Joe and Barb bought my round trip ticket to get me there and back. They called us over one night for dinner and told us that they believe in our vision and want to get involved. Then they said they would buy my ticket and loan us a car in the interim. Also, there was a couple, Frank and Marilyn Nelson, (the ones with the "self-cleaning" dog.), who made a sacrifice and passed on buying a personal item for Marilyn to give us something. Altogether, Dorothy and I split up the seven hundred dollars we had which would have to sustain us both for the month while I was gone. I would be traveling to Heathrow

Airport outside of London, England. I would find my way somehow across Europe to Slovenia, prepare a means for us to live, and return to England a month later for the return flight, all on less than four hundred dollars. I refrain from saying "What an idiot!" because I wouldn't want to dampen this great story of faith, yet it can well be imagined what many of our relatives thought of me then (and now, too, I suppose).

I knew that if I were to make such a move, I would have to see our church leadership about it. I was nervous, as our pastoral staff was known for their protective caution. They were charismatic, but no one ever accused them of moving out too quickly. I decided that I would speak to no one but our head pastor, Wayne Benson. I didn't want the possibility of anyone confusing the issue with different suggestions or doubts before I spoke with "the big guy" himself. I was primed and "prayed-up," as some used to say. I had decided that if he specifically said "no," then I would can the whole thing and stay put.

When we had a few minutes at the end of an evening service, Dorothy and I sat with him and his wife in the pew. He listened intently, as he always did until I was finished with a summary of my calling and desire to serve God. When I was done, there was silence for a few moments. When he slowly said, "God could be calling you to go to Slovenia..." my heart leaped because he didn't say "No." He gave some advice about seeking God and encouraged me to ask myself some hard questions, but said little else. This was unbelievable, a miracle even. I was sure he would have vigorously tried to stop me, so I had prayed that day God would speak directly to him. Pastor Benson never said whether or not he had heard from God about me, but I was convinced that God had told him to neither bless, nor curse my calling.

I believe that when a person sets out to do something in the Spirit of God but is not recognized by his local fellowship, there are some potential problems and dangers that can arise. Perhaps the greatest of these is not only that there are many wolves in sheep's clothing around the church, leading people astray of the truth, a person could find himself becoming such a self-serving "wolf" if he does not take care to keep a deep commitment to the body of Christ.

We have, therefore always been very careful to remain in church fellowship wherever we go. When we moved to Slovenia we remained quiet members of the church where Steve Telzerow was pastoring and did not proclaim ourselves in any way to other churches or leaders. On occasion, when invited, we went to meet brothers and sisters in other churches, but in no way did we ever represent ourselves as having been sent by any church or organization in the United States. The only exception was when witnessing to our un-churched neighbors who wanted to know where we were from and why we were there.

Likewise, in Germany. From the first Sunday we lived in Munich we have attended the same charismatic church and became members as soon as possible. At no time in Slovenia or Germany did we do anything bringing correction from church leadership. When a few of the members of the Slovenian church suggested eldership for me, Steve Telzerow and I talked and decided that it would not be a good idea for me to hold a position of authority. Neither have I sought any such position of authority in Germany. In fact, I refused an offer to become assistant pastor in a charismatic church we visited where I preached a few times.

All of this relates to what God has called us to do, and what He hasn't called us to do. It's probably true that God called me to become a missionary pastor when I was much younger. For many reasons, mostly selfish ones, I didn't answer that calling until very late in the game. I was not obedient to God, and I believe it cost me something. If God wants me to pastor a church, I am willing, but He will have to move in that direction first. I am sure that at this time God wants us to find people who are doing His work but are discouraged, weary, or in transition. We will encourage, support, and give in whatever ways we find to be helpful. This includes praying, singing, giving money, visiting, talking, preaching, teaching, and making coffee. My wife often says that we are to be like those two men who held up Moses' arms during a great battle on the way to the Promised Land. Whenever we find un-churched people who are interested in knowing about God, we witness as best as we can, making every effort to bring them into the local fellowship.

Sometimes, the difficulties keeping us from doing God's will are not at all what they seem. We certainly thought that the children's schooling would be a problem in the mission field, that homeschooling was our only possibility. In the end we saw that schooling was not a problem at all; only we couldn't have known it until we arrived. Dorothy had been teaching the children from a homeschooling curriculum since they were old enough to go to school. There was quite a bit of support from other homeschoolers, and the children were on such a distinctly higher level than the neighbors, some of them went so far as to buy home school materials to supplement the public education of their own kids.

So we naturally thought that homeschooling was the answer to the problem of education in a foreign land, so when we arrived in Ljubljana in June 1997, one of the ten boxes we brought contained enough home school materials for one more year of instruction. We still have the books, although we haven't ever used them.

Immediately after renting a house in Dragomer, just outside Ljubljana in mid-August, just a couple months after arriving in Slovenia, our kids aired their opinion to Dorothy with a united voice: "We want to go to school." They absolutely refused to be dissuaded, it was incredible.

I thought that it was a simple case of them not understanding what they would be facing. Slovenia had been a free republic for only six years, and so the people generally did not speak English. Our kids had never gone to school in the United States; how would they possibly enter a foreign school? Their reply was as compelling as it was firm. They told Dorothy, "Mom, we are not just missionary kids, but we are kid missionaries."

At their insistence, Dorothy went to the school before the academic year began and talked with the principle, while Barbara Telzerow was kind enough to translate. The principal said that the experience would be good for the Slovenian kids as well as ours. I think that she felt she was giving our kids a break because they had never heard of homeschooling before and were afraid that it was harmful to our children.

It was a strange day, indeed, when Dorothy and I loaded up their backpacks and took them to school, leaving them there alone while we walked back home. It took a little over half an hour to get home by foot, a nice walk past cute rural houses with tile roofs and a few old barns separated by hay fields, not to mention the masses of snails and slugs, with an occasional snake thrown in.

At first, the people of the village (and school) thought we were part of some odd cult. As time went on and we used the word "missionary," they decided we must be Mormons. Finally, they arrived at the understanding we were some kind of Christian, but they didn't know what kind. In Slovenia, the word "Christian" usually means "Catholic," while the word "Protestant" usually means Lutheran. Anyone who is not a

Catholic or a Lutheran or perhaps a Mormon must either be an atheist or a member of a cult.

I will never cease to be amazed at the learning ability of our children. It's hard for me to say exactly how the kids learned so well that they achieved passing grades in all subjects in the Slovene language by the end of the first school year. They were definitely immersed in the language. Candace was the only one who had a teacher with more than rudimentary English skills. As I remember, the first words and sentences they learned were part of a game they often played with friends. The game is called "gummi twist," or "Chinese jump rope."

Only a week after the beginning of the school year, Amanda went on a class trip. At first, we were a bit nervous because we heard the trip would be to Croatia. Our new friends quickly set our minds at ease about the safety of Croatia (remember the war.). After all, they convinced us, their destination was just an hour or so over the border on the coast.

51

All the same, we didn't tell our relatives in the United States about it until a later time. So, Amanda traveled across the border without us for seven days, not able to speak the language. We sure did pray that all would be well, but there was nothing to worry about. The school made these trips every year without incident, and if any questions would have arisen at the border, Amanda's teacher planned to tell the officials that she was Amanda's relative, to explain the forty Slovenian passports with one American thrown in. It's difficult to explain the feelings of security and warmth we experienced whenever we were around the Slovenian teachers and their schoolchildren. We later found that Amanda's teacher had been very motherly to her on the trip. She took her into the teacher's room to sleep when she felt insecure and even took her to a private get together with her personal friends who were vacationing in their mobile home in the area. (They were happy to have Amanda, as she was the first American they had ever met.)

When Amanda returned, she gave an excellent report about how fun it had been, swimming and sketching marine life. One of her teachers wanted to know more about her Christianity, too. We had been in Slovenia only four months, and we were already witnessing Jesus to someone who would not typically have visited the church we attended.

Within a couple of weeks, the children all had friends in the school in Dragomer. The girls even participated in the cheerleading for boys' basketball. They made some friends on the cheerleading squad, too. This "sport" is different from what it used to be in my time; now, it seems to be quite a gymnastic event. When they began, the squad was pretty green, but an excellent gymnastics teacher, Katarina, coached it. Dorothy became the assistant coach and got to know her very well, helping organize a summer camp for the girls, like they do in the United States. (Dorothy had been a cheerleader in high school, and made good use of her experience). Katarina took the idea of a summer practice camp and perfected it by making the arrangements for the Adriatic Coast, which was only two hours away by bus. The summer camp was so fun as well as useful they return every year. In 1999, the team finished first in the Slovenian national competition. The fun part for Dorothy and the girls was that every year since we left Slovenia, they were invited again to go with the team to the coast for the summer camp.

As fun as it all is in the ancient city of Piran (Dorothy saw an 800-year-old church), not a single trip happened in which someone didn´t want to talk about Jesus, and what our family believes and why we are in Europe. Amanda once talked a friend through her suicidal feelings (the top cause of teenage death in Slovenia), and Dorothy finally got onc of the schoolteachers to start coming to our church. Without warning, at no particular time, kids or teachers would ask our children about their faith and the church they attend; they were always ready. At camp, Dorothy witnessed to every teacher, at one time or another.

It was also common for the Slovenian kids to talk about "those Americans" to their parents. Many times we had invitations to visit with parents, who eventually would talk with us about why we were there. These are people who had no interest in going to church or talking with people doing street evangelism. It took time to get to know them a little before we could speak to them to any significant depth.

The Slovenians are highly developed socially. Some of my students told me that in the communist days, which ended only six or seven years earlier, everyone had work, a place to live, and food, but few had extra money for spending on travel. So, they generally stayed home, except for the summer migration to the coast, where many shared inexpensive mobile summer homes or cabins. The daily routine, therefore, was that both parents would leave early for work after sending their kids to school. Some of them dropped the kids off as early as 5:30 in the morning. These kids would sleep at school for an hour or so until it was time to get ready for class. The younger kids would be left with grandma and grandpa until mom and dad came home. The late afternoon, evening, and nighttime were spent at home, so the neighbors got to know each other very well, especially considering that people so rarely moved that very many of the people we knew were living in houses their grandparents lived in when they were young or built themselves. So, the neighbors took turns spending half the day in each other's homes.

We found it was difficult to make a short visit with friends or neighbors. Where we come from, it is possible to "just drop in" on someone for half an hour to an hour at a time for coffee and a doughnut. Not so, in Slovenia, where when we went to see someone, we found that if it was after three o´clock in the afternoon, we would be there until seven or eight, and would have had at least one meal. Once, when I said to our host, "thank you for having us over," she looked a little surprised and asked me if that was some kind of American greeting. She told me that there, people say "thank you for coming to my home." Everyone assumes that people will make invitations, but not everyone will cross town to visit.

We began to learn early about differences in social customs and manners. If we went for a visit, for example, and offered to help clean up, people would sometimes be offended. Also, we quickly learned to never pay a visit without a token gift such as a small bag of coffee, chocolate, candy, or a flower.

To this day, when we make visits back to Slovenia, we are still warmly welcomed in the school by the teachers, helpers, and even the principal. Some of our kids´ old schoolmates continue to invite our kids to come and see them.

The move of God's Holy Spirit through us in Slovenia is connected with the revival in Grand Rapids, which we participated in, and so, indirectly connected, with the Brownsville Revival. We have been so changed by these things we cannot go back to Michigan and resume our regular lives, working and attending church like before. We cannot turn our backs on God and His plans for our lives that He revealed over these past few years. We look at each other sometimes and say, "we're ruined for anything else."

In my recollection, the revival at First Assembly started to form in December 1995 when Pastor Benson found he could not preach his usual sermon, as the Spirit of God prevented him. For several weeks, this man who usually had sermons planned long in advance was stopped without a clear idea as to what was happening. In the following months, the pastors visited Brownsville, Florida, to see firsthand what was taking place. By father's day (the anniversary of the first day of revival services in Florida), First Assembly was in revival. It began during a few services in which the pastors led the people to prayerfully consider their lives and then come to the front, kneel and pray about anything requiring confession. In this environment, with thousands of people praying and confessing sins, the Spirit of God quickly began moving. Shortly following, signs started happening such as men returning to their wives, teenagers leaving gang activity to return home, relatives who never were interested in church suddenly coming to Jesus, people being physically healed, and so on.

For us, though, the revival probably really began more than a year before though we didn't know what it was and what would eventually happen. A girl in Sunday school who was around the age of eight fell "under the power of the Spirit" in the junior worship service, led by Pastor Rich LaBelle. This happened sometimes in Sunday school, but more often among the adults. This time, though, this girl stayed there for more than one hour, hardly moving. When she woke up, she told about how she was in heaven, where she, Jesus, and her father walked, talked, and ate together. Her father had been killed in a construction accident when she was very young.

From that time forward, these kinds of visions were more and more commonplace among the children. Before long, some services saw dozens of kids around the ages of eight to twelve lying on the floor, crying, laughing, being silent, or praying. I was brought up in the Baptist church and continued in that doctrine until I was in my early twenties. In that church, we young people had always believed that miracles and speaking in tongues happened in the world, but that they were limited to those who "really" needed them, and often talked about miracles in the mission field.

To me, as a boy, that meant people who lived in jungles and, for all I knew, ate bugs and faced natives with poison darts; it wasn't to be until I grew up and found out what the word "need" can mean. For example, sometime in the middle of the night when my one-year-old daughter had a high fever and was dehydrated and vomiting, I thought differently about the list of people who "need" God to move miraculously.

One girl in my Sunday school class provides an excellent example of what went on with the children in the Spirit. We Sunday school teachers were praying for the children one-day at the front of the service. A girl who was about eleven came forward for me to pray. She said she would like prayer for anger; she was feeling every day against her family. I wouldn't have thought that there could be anything serious in such a sweet-looking young girl. I placed my hand on her head and began to pray in the Spirit. After a few moments, I sensed some relaxing in her. A moment later, her body grew rigid, and she fell over, not bending as I laid her on the floor. I was quite stunned; although I had prayed for kids before, this was a first. When the girl got up, she was so happy; I began to see a little of why she wanted prayer. Before her experience, she seemed like a normal, quiet, healthy girl, but at this moment, she was normal, healthy, and filled with joy. Afterward, when I saw her free and happy I knew that her previous condition was not normal; she was heavier at heart than she needed to be.

As the adult service became like the children's service, with people praising at the front and dancing during the service, I found myself beginning to hunger for more of His presence that I had previously known. Dorothy had always been someone who sought more and more from God in very open and expressive ways. Now it wasn't that I didn't want more of God; I just believed for decades that the Christian attitude should be an attitude of quiet humility and reflection. All too often, however, it was an excuse for being withdrawn. It was easy enough to love people, but I usually never really got close to people or allowed then to get close to me. The Bible says, "open rebuke is better than "hidden love." I was growing to an understanding of the potential waste of a withdrawn life. Before I was finished, I would eventually trade everything I had for the opportunity to go out and give love to those who needed it. For the time being, I was struggling to really "feel," as my wife always says.

Dorothy was among the first on most occasions to get into worship and praise. She found it natural to dive into discussions about Jesus with almost everyone in her life, from the "pizza man" to some stranger she just met in the government office while getting her license renewed. It's more than just being gregarious; she has always lived with her life on display. It's just out there for everyone to see, for me, I had a lot of difficulty being open like that.

I remember services with either Pastor Benson or the revival evangelist, Sam Rijfkogel praying for the people. I would look around and see hundreds of people lying on the floor, twitching and crying and laughing, usually all at the same time. I remember seeing all this because I was always left standing. Like a single tree in the middle of a vast plain, I was beginning to worry about myself, "am I such a cold fish that I can´t receive?" and "what is all this about; is it necessary?" For months I was left standing, probably for many reasons, but God was at work.

One day, instead of remaining the only upright body, I felt a sort of anticipation as the pastor moved toward me. People were falling by the dozen, and as he approached me, I felt something rise up from the floor, like the surge of a great wave, and I fell over on my back. It was funny because I remember being amused by the fact that I could get up any time, but I didn´t want to. My family said later that I was quite funny, lying on the floor, twitching and laughing (I don't remember this part).

After that time, I fell on other occasions, certainly not all; I was freed from the nagging worry that something was wrong. I found that this being "in the Spirit" was not so strange or weird as I had thought. It was actually all quite natural. One of the times, I had quite a different experience. I had an impression of an outdoor scene in a wooded area by a lake. There were trees, leaves, grass, and other everyday things found outside, like flowers. Jesus came and picked up a green leaf. He told me that He was the designer. He could tell me about the physics of the leaf, as well as the chemistry, the mathematics, and certainly the biology. "But," I understood, "there is plenty of time later to look into these things together. I want you to please leave these things behind because people are dying in need of help and salvation. People have limited time and cannot be dealt with later. Please spend your time on people rather than things. Time is so short for so many."

As the revival progressed, I became more and more certain that I no longer wished to pursue my career in automobile quality assurance. I wanted to "go out" and find someone who had real needs that I could help. All of the motivational, fire breathing sermons I had heard in the decades of my church attendance rested upon me like a great weight. How many times did someone say "there's no safer place than being than out on a limb with God." How many times did the choir sing a song with the phrase "go to them"? How many times did I hear a preacher admonish the people to get "out of the pews and into the streets"? All my life, I heard these sayings and thought little about them. I had always tried to capitalize on opportunities in the workplace when they arose, but the amount of opportunity in my life never matched the testimonies of the people who were trying to help the church to see life from a different perspective.

Now that I was waking up to a new perspective on the world, a perspective in which "the world" really mattered, not just my corner of it. I wanted to live differently. I was on fire to live for once. To see the world as it is, I had to make certain conclusions about my hometown. The fact is that Grand Rapids, Michigan, USA, is so churched that, at one time, I heard it had more churches per person than any other city in the world. In my hometown, the gospel of Jesus Christ is the dominant theme of Christian preaching. Somewhere, Christians were supposedly preaching "new age" style sermons in their worldliness, but for me, I found the message of salvation through faith in Jesus Christ to be everywhere, from roadside billboards to vacation bible school at the local Lutheran church, to the three local Christian radio channels. If I wanted to answer the great commission, I knew that it was improbable that God was sending me to Grand Rapids

I knew from many years of being in church that there were places in the world where either few Christians lived or where the life had gone out of the church. One such place, which fascinated me, was middle Europe, the very cradle of the reformation and modern Christianity. My heart burned when I heard of how nothing new had been happening for many years.

At that time, I had very little information about the former iron curtain countries, but I supposed there was a real need there. Of course, I knew that I had never taken any formal or official training for the ministry, and I was sure that I was not ready to go to very difficult places. My heart was, however, that with Europe supposedly spiritually stagnant, here I was, living a Christian life in the United States. If a person like me moved to Europe, then the people in my life could be enriched, learning from me what I had learned from our ministers, even if

I led a reasonably ordinary life. Over time I could prepare for more formal ministry.

Before we left, the anointing that was on Dorothy became more and more apparent, such that, after observing the Holy Spirit move through Dorothy when she prayed for people at the front of some of the services, Sam, the revival preacher, often invited her to follow him and pray for people as he laid hands on them and prayed. Sometimes people would receive a word from God through Dorothy, and sometimes people were filled with the Holy Spirit. Not wishing for any rumor of impropriety, the elders of our church decided that Dorothy should not work with Sam directly, but rather with one of the church elders who always ministered together with his wife.

They thought that it was a good idea to involve me, so the four of us prayed for a lot of people together. This was all new to me, not so much praying in the Spirit, because I had done that before, but the somewhat humble position of following people who were "really anointed," when I was there only because I was the Spirit-filled husband of someone who was ministering. I must have been changing because, in the past, I'm sure I would have thought it beneath me, or too embarrassing that I wasn't the leader. At that time, however, I was just grateful to God to be at all involved, seeing that there had been times in my life when I put personal priorities ahead of the hand of God. It would have been fair enough for God to put me on a shelf somewhere, but that's not the way He is. Besides, there is a lot of work in this world to be done, and not so many people who are willing to do it. If every community in the world had a fully supported pastor, I'd be back in the automobile industry.

Once, when the elder Brian White prayed for us, he became a little disturbed, then prayed that God would keep us safe. He said God was showing him that we were five small lambs, held securely in His hand. This was so significant to us, at a time when we were planning to go to some unknown foreign land, that Dorothy made a "praise hoop," a sort of tambourine rim with an embroidered cloth scene on it, with shining streamers hanging from the rim. The scene she painted was one of a hand with five lambs in it; it still hangs on our wall in the entryway to our apartment. When anyone asks what it is, they get the whole story, because it certainly has become true that God has kept His hand on us in every circumstance, whether people failed us or not.

When I went to Slovenia in April 1997, for a "spying out" trip to gather information on moving my family there, I did not know what to expect. I believed that there were people who needed encouragement, but I had no idea how I would meet such people or what I could do for them

Steve and Barbara Telzerow were so completely kind and accepting that I keep them in mind as an example of how to encourage others. They helped me to seek God and trust Him, without passing judgment where they might have thought I was crazy, nor by encouraging me to move apart from the church. Steve took me virtually everywhere with him that month, as he went about his routine pastoral visits and attended his ordinary prayer meetings and such. I met more people than I can remember names, and more and more I felt sure that my life had come alive. I realized full force the futility of many things I used to think necessary and the importance of individual people in various places who had needs for which I didn't need to be a theologian to touch.

When that first Sunday in Slovenia came, I was in for a great surprise. As there had been a pulling apart in the church, leading to a split, Steve had been advised by his overseer to stand aside until everything settled, (Steve at that time was assisting the Slovenian pastor). For a few months directly previous to my visit, he had not been attending the Sunday gathering, now in a house rather than the church. I also didn't know that many members of the church were feeling like they were forgotten by God, as punishment for leaving their fellowship where they felt stifled. They were seeking God's will and were confessing their sins and leaving their hearts open for God's direction right up to the very Sunday that I arrived. That Sunday, Steve was not present when friends took me to the service.

As I arrived at the house where the homegroup was meeting in the evening, I heard the music coming from the living room. The room was packed with people, and there was a very tangible sense of God's Holy Spirit. After many warm greetings, the worship service began. I was moved in my heart in a way I had never experienced. Although I am usually a very self-conscious person, I couldn't help but to cry without being able to stop, though the music consisted of only one or two guitars and people singing, I felt as though it were the most powerful music I had ever heard. Something extraordinary was happening, but I didn't know quite what it was all about. When it was finished, the people expected my testimony, specifically about the revival. Most of the people in the room spoke some English, but a translator was required, something new for me.

As I related what I had seen and heard during the revival services in Grand Rapids, and a few words about what I thought it all meant, I was often overcome and cried some while I talked. It was so emotional, it was hard to continue, and thinking back, I feel embarrassed, but at the time it seemed natural. I told them about Amanda's visions of heaven and Jesus and about things children in Sunday school had testified, as well as impressions from the adult revival services, how marriages had been restored, and wayward children had returned home. When I finished, I was greatly distressed to find that they expected me to lead them in a Holy Spirit anointing oil service. This was something that I did not feel equal to in any way. What happened to the idea that I would just come to Europe and live a "normal" life for a while? This wasn't the least bit funny. I prayed, "God, these people have a need and expect something; I'm here, and you're here, so please meet their needs through me today, for your sake, in spite of me."

As the music played, I anointed each person with oil and prayed, mostly in the Spirit. To my amazement, some of the people went down onto the couch, some broke down crying, and one person saw a vision. She spoke no English, and I didn't understand at first what she was talking about for a few minutes. She asked everyone to explain to her who the man was she had just seen. When questioned in depth by the Slovenians there, she told how she was somewhere near quiet water where she saw a man, tall and fatherly, who walked with her and held her hand. He was so loving and gentle; she had a great desire to know him and to stay with him. As the people told her it must be Jesus, she asked for more knowledge. She had accepted Jesus a short time before but knew only a little about Him.

The people said they were so encouraged that they felt God was telling them that they were not forgotten. They were built up and felt much more like continuing as a church, rather than going off separately to find some other church.

When I returned to Steve and Barbara's house, they were waiting for me. I don't know if anyone had called ahead to tell them about the service, but they were very attentive to what I had to relate. Then, to my surprise, they asked if I would anoint them and pray, too. I was intimidated because Steve was an ordained AG minister, but I suppose that until that moment, I had assumed that whenever the Holy Spirit moves, He moves first and most through the leadership. This is a general principle I still hold to, but I could see that I wasn't giving enough consideration to the humanity of a minister. I was encouraged to see that there are ways a person like myself can bring encouragement, and there are times when an established minister can receive something from an "ordinary Christian." This was vital for me to understand, as I planned to base my future on it. Anyway, they were also filled with the Spirit and fell out on the floor. That left just me standing there alone, wondering what God would want to do through me if I were willing.

All in all, it is interesting to see the hand of God move through mere men, knowing that He does not need us, but prefers to work through us, for our benefit over and above the blessing He wants someone else to receive. It is also interesting to note that the revival in Grand Rapids was often described as a move of God, which was to be transferred through personal contact to other people, fellowships, and ministers in various places, near and far. Sam had prayed more than once in the revival as he laid hands on us that we would "take the fire" to Europe. I did not doubt God had moved, person-to-person, from the prophecy of a South Korean minister (Pastor Cho), to a medium-sized church in Florida (Pastor Kilpatrick), to a big church in Grand Rapids (Pastor Benson), through me to a small group of people in a house outside Ljubljana, Slovenia (Pastor Telzerow), who were calling out to God to move in their lives. This was really living!

This was just the beginning. When Dorothy and the kids came to Slovenia with me I found out what being charismatic was all about. At times, God will use me in a dramatic way, like in that anointing service, but in our family, I am the one who teaches and stays calm, sorting out problems and giving instructions. Dorothy is the one who moves consistently in physically expressive ways.

From nearly the first day in Slovenia, God showed us how He wanted to work not only in typical ways like talking to people and teaching but also in dramatic, charismatic ways. I don't remember how it started, but when I think of it, I do remember that Dorothy and Barbara moved similarly, often at the same time. If one of them began to pray, they would both get that charismatic bowing I saw people doing in the revival. When one of them would start doing that, the other involuntarily started doing it, too, complete with very loud groans and even wailing. At first, I must say it was a little unnerving to hear. I don't like things that call attention to us, and this sort of thing was not very inconspicuous.

Here I was, in the home of a minister, and my wife was making quite a spectacle. On the other hand, as I asked God to show me what He was doing, keeping my mind open after all that we had seen in the revival services in Grand Rapids, I could find no fault; it was simply different from my previous experience. Who was I to complain that God was moving? It became funny at times because Steve and I are a little more alike, and Barbara and Dorothy are a bit more alike. We four would be at the table having lunch or something when Dorothy or Barbara would start making a groaning sound, and that was it. They would both end up on the floor, on at least one occasion immersed in almost uncontrollable laughter. In the meantime, Steve and I remained at the table, maybe talking, maybe quiet, waiting to see what God was up to. We didn't begin moving like Dorothy and Barbara. I was glad that I wasn't the only one who was a little less expressive physically; it made me feel more sure that the manifestation of God's hand could be different from person to person, even depending on something so trivial as a personality. I kept an open mind, all along though, and sometimes I wished I was a little more like Dorothy, and a little less logical, sometimes I was just glad to be me.

This sort of thing occurred almost daily over the ten or twelve weeks we stayed with the Telzerows. I quickly understood that I was no longer in the pew in Grand Rapids, Michigan. Another time, Dorothy and I were downstairs, getting the laundry ready when Barbara came down to do the same. As soon as Barbara passed Dorothy, one of them let out a loud "ooh" and that was it; both were on the floor once again. When Steve came, we ended up praying, and Dorothy said God wanted to say that "these groans were the birth pains of a revival in Slovenia."

Those weeks in the Telzerow home were special, like no other time in my life. I would have liked to remain with them for a very long time, praying and talking, enjoying the things that God brought about in our fellowship. I know, though, that the experience was not entirely unlike the experience Peter had on the mountain when Jesus was transfigured. He was having a special time together with Jesus, but God had work for him to do, which was less dramatic, may have seemed less spiritual but was more critical. God had people whose lives needed to be touched. Peter was to leave his safe mountaintop experience, and we were to move out into our own home

In a short time, with Slavko's help, we rented a house a couple of villages toward town from Steve and Barbara. The daily revival fires we had been experiencing gave way to a more normal routine, what with school for the kids, and work for me. With a more normal life, though, came regular and varied opportunities to witness of Jesus to people who did not know Him; Dorothy, being both more outgoing and pleasant, as well as being home while I was at work, worked herself in with the neighbors quite quickly.

Watching Dorothy with the neighbors, discussing major gardening theory with only a couple hundred common words for communication, I was reminded of what I knew but what did not come easily for me in my past. That is, people are touched through genuine caring and love. That idea, as a concept, is simple enough. The execution of that idea is not only where people fail; it is where the meaning of life resides. Countless times I would be somewhere with Dorothy, such as the vegetable stand down the road, going about my everyday business. We would be ready to leave, but Dorothy was engaged in conversation with someone working there. Sometimes there would be an invitation for coffee, sometimes some other meeting, sometimes nothing. The discussions were usually not particularly in-depth or important. Half the time, people talked about their relationships or worries. I learned from Dorothy how vital everyday matters are because they matter to people we love.

The result of some of the street ministry we joined in Ljubljana, or that Dorothy joined while I was working was that she knew several of the local bums by name. Often, when we walked through the city center, we would see one of them. Now, honestly, I'm not repulsed by these people, but in the past I would not have thought to try to talk to them, assuming they wouldn't be affected by anything I could say, me being from such a "straight" background. Not Dorothy, though, no way.

She would get them into the same conversations that we had with more "respectable" people. They all had hopes and fears, relationships that were going either poorly or improving, and I learned what I might have known in my head but not my heart, that people are the same, regardless of condition. Some have it better, and some have it worse, that's all.

One day while Dorothy was attending the all-day teacher training sessions at Berlitz, I dropped in to teach a class. The training supervisor told me: "Hey, do you know that your wife said she spent her lunchtime with the bums today?" I thought for a moment and then said, "that sounds like her." The supervisor was left speechless.

Around Christmas, when we were in the United States for my father's funeral, people from our church visited the "Hell Motel," an abandoned building where many bums and druggies slept when it was cold. As they explained what they wanted to do, one of the bums asked, "Do you know Dorothy?"

Our friend from the church replied, "Yes, Dorothy is one of us, but she isn't here right now." The bum said, „then you can come in."

The reason I think Dorothy can make these connections is that she genuinely doesn't care what people think about her. It's not that she loves people, and I don't, because I do, but it's more like she breaks all unwritten rules of society to show she cares, and some people appreciate it. If we use the underground here in Munich, and some woman smiles at our children or at something we say, (which indicates they speak some English), I smile back but remain silent like everyone else. Not Dorothy, no way. She busts out with some silly remark, which immediately gets people into a conversation or at least into laughter. Sometimes, they laugh out loud and have a good time, breaking up the monotony (and silence) of the business hour subway crowd. It's incredible what a little change in perspective can bring with it.

When I hear from Dorothy about the illness of some child, the daughter of a woman who is sister to some friend of ours, knowing the child's name, and actually knowing much about the family, simply because her friend had told her about them at some earlier time, I gain some understanding about what makes Dorothy so different.

I know her very well after fifteen years of marriage, and I can confidently say she doesn't have an exceptional memory. She does take a genuine interest in things that I wouldn't want to hear about, much less remember. When I think about it, I don't conclude that she cares more about people than me, but she does see people from a more every day, down to earth perspective. Whereas I might be thinking about what makes a person the way he is from a philosophical or functional point of view, Dorothy "feels" with them, regardless of how trivial the subject may seem. What is important to a friend is important to Dorothy. When a friend grieves over the loss of a pet dog, I listen but think to myself, "it's just a dog." Not so, Dorothy, she listens less to the facts and empathizes more with the person grieving. "She is sad," Dorothy might think, "I feel for her."

Sometimes, Dorothy's spiritual openness is a little scary. When God tells her to do something, there is no time for rationalizing or considering (or even planning); she is off in a moment. We all visited an associated charismatic church in Ljubljana several times. The first time Dorothy met Pastor Daniel, I was with our kids who were sick. I would naturally keep my reserve when meeting a minister, not knowing his disposition. When Dorothy shook his hand, however, God spoke a word to her for him. I heard it was quite comical because the moment their hands closed, Dorothy was overcome by the power of the Holy Spirit and started bowing, gripping his hand even tighter. She spoke the word to him (actually I was told she shouted) then he reacted with trembling and tears, also overcome. When it was finished, they released their hands, and he had met Dorothy! He said he was very encouraged and has been very warm to us ever since. In this way, Dorothy has become quite well known in Slovenian charismatic circles between Ljubljana and the coast. On the other hand, the few times I delivered a word from God to the church, the people were very attentive because I don't frequently move in that gift, and they had the idea something special was happening.

The year after we moved to Germany, Steve and Barbara were in the United States all year, itinerating. I knew that the Slovenian elders were competent, but when I heard they were becoming tired, I developed a burden for them and the people in general. That year, 1999, I traveled to Ljubljana by train at least half a dozen times to preach and teach. I have always said that our mission in Europe is to assist and encourage whenever and wherever we can. I was delighted to be able to preach but was also nervous. It was uncomfortable for me. Therefore, every time I taught, God spoke to my heart and modified, completed, or changed my message during the worship service directly before the sermon.

I often hear the voice of God very clearly in corporate worship services. In Slovenia, the service usually was the first opportunity I had to pray with the members of the church before preaching. I would often take the train leaving Munich Hauptbahnhof at 11:45 p.m. on Friday, arriving at 6:00 am. Then, I would leave at either 4:00 or 10:30 p.m. Sunday to arrive back in Munich either late at night or early in the morning. Once, I arrived at 6:00 am Monday, caught a subway home, showered, and was off to teach a lesson by eight. I love my adventures on the train very much, and can't wait to go again as soon as possible.

I always thought, probably because of old movies, people who travel by train in Europe take a lot of baggage. In fact, however, there is no room provided even on long-distance trains other than a shelf overhead for a briefcase or something.

When we returned to Slovenia after my father's funeral in December 1997, we brought ten large boxes (the maximum size for airline check-in), a guitar, a violin, camera, four pillows, a purse and five soft bags that were airline carry-on. We landed in Munich and had to take the train to Ljubljana. It wasn't so simple; we had to take the "S-Bahn" (metro) from the airport to the Hauptbahnhof (central train station) then get on the train. Getting the S-Bahn was not a problem, although we did take up a large section of the train car.

Five minutes before the train was to leave, I decided that we were on the wrong train, so I very quickly moved all of those things across the platform to the other train. Later I would learn that both trains would get me to the Hauptbahnhof, as the airport was an end station. Forty-five minutes later, I must have looked strange to the locals at the Hauptbahnhof because 99.9% of the people on an S-Bahn carry next to nothing as it's chiefly used to get to and from work. If we hadn't gotten Johanna to bring some of the things in her car from the airport, we might have unknowingly lost some bags as the S-Bahn door stays open for only a half-minute or so at each stop.

At the escalator, I was like a squirrel and his nuts. There were no elevators because I got off on the wrong side of the train (and didn't know about the elevators). I took one box up two escalators and set it down, quickly came back for half of the family, back for boxes, and so on, until all boxes and family were upstairs where the intercity trains were. Johanna and her mother were there at the station to help, and her mom even brought food. While we waited for the train, I became quite nervous because it was increasingly apparent that the train would pull in and out within a couple of minutes. Later we would find out that large amounts of baggage must be pre-loaded on a cargo car. The result was that in our haste to get everything and everyone on the train, Dorothy and I and

Johanna loaded our stuff in record time, but in different cars, as quite a mass of people boarded the train. Once underway, I took twenty minutes transferring things from my car through the aisles to Dorothy´s car. People seemed quite amused by watching the Americans struggle with such an everyday event as riding the train.

Before long, we found that the train wasn´t scheduled to travel straight through to Ljubljana. In a couple of hours, the train we were on would stop for precisely three minutes, while the train we were to catch would leave less than five minutes later. At least, as far as we could figure, the second train would be departing from a parallel track. While I sat and wondered, trying the think of what to do, Dorothy walked up and down the aisle, recruiting men who would help unload our things during the three-minute stop.

It went well, considering that nobody was willing to get off the train for such a short stop. When the train ground to a halt, I leaped off, turned around, and had four men handing me boxes and bags nonstop, from a doorway and three windows, until all was unloaded. Thirty seconds later, the train was off, everyone on the car was laughing and waving, and I rushed to get the things onto the next train over before it left, frantic to confirm from a schedule written in German that it was the correct train. When I finished with a minute or so to spare, thanks to a helpful train conductor, I was beat. Finally, less than an hour later, we felt like we were home again when we reached the Slovenian border.

The Slovenian policija (police) are always friendly while they check passports. Usually, they will chat a little with Americans. Then, men in brown uniforms marked "Carina" boarded; they were the customs inspectors. There was nothing friendly or funny about them. They asked, with grave expressions, after several attempts in both Slovene and German, "You have something...uh...declare?" The dumb American (me) answered "no" because I thought they were only interested in cigarettes, alcohol, and such for tax purposes. I didn't mention the massive pile of things around the corner because it was all our personal property, and none of it was even new.

After they went out, I talked with Dorothy a little and began to wonder what they might have meant. I had a funny feeling, so I went out to check our things around the corner. What I found was four brown suited Carina preparing to unload our boxes. Wrong answer! When I stopped them and motioned that those things were mine, three of them turned on me in anger, apparently using the one remaining English sentence they knew, "You said nothing... declare." They repeated it with increasing intensity as I tried to use my brother's formula for surviving overseas, "just smile, and everything will be all right." It wasn't working, and they seemed perplexed that one person would have so many things on the train.

I was the only American on board. I was getting nervous, picturing all sorts of ugly, drawn-out scenes involving fines or jail, all somewhere other than on the train. "Just make sure we stay on the train," I thought. A moment later, one of the men said something short and sharp. Immediately, two men cut open four out of ten boxes and rifled through the potpourri of various personal items. They must have expected something else, because they quickly calmed down and before I knew it, they all jumped off the train without another word, good or bad, and without repacking my stuff.

As I crunched down our stuff and closed the boxes, the train started rolling, and I stopped sweating, breathed more comfortable, and after realizing I had been sweating and breathing heavily, I relaxed. When I returned to our compartment, trying to be cool, I interrupted quite a little prayer service!

One day, Dorothy was singing in Slovene with the homegroup. Slovene is easy to pronounce, as it is entirely phonetic. Somewhere in the middle of a song she said a word like "noznica," but it should have been "mnozica." All at once everyone was laughing. The music stopped, with tears rolling down some of the women's' cheeks. When everyone stopped slapping their sides and giggling, someone leaned over to Dorothy and told her that the word she used had less to do with the character of God as it did with some part of the female anatomy. If we didn't have humility before, we were learning it now.

We went to visit a family early on, our first "solo" visit with Slovenians other than members of Barbara's family. We felt very adventurous. It was funny because we fell into the old error of assuming dinner was between five and seven in the evening. As we were to arrive at five, we were sure that dinner was part of the invitation. The Slovenians often eat their big meal much earlier in the day, however, sometimes as early as three in the afternoon. So, it was our mistake, but there was no food. There were snacking munchies set out (mostly involving chocolate), as well as Turkish coffee (robust). When we ate all of the chocolate covered cookies, they refilled the bowl with something else, like chips. The kids were hungry, so they ate all of those, too. When our hosts went into the kitchen to look around and found something else to fill the bowl with, I started to get the idea.

When the nuts were gone, they went to find whatever was left; I realized that no matter how many times we ate what they put out, they would get something else. When they went into the kitchen together the fourth time, I quickly told my kids to make sure they didn't eat any more, or at least to leave some in the bowl. I promised them pizza when we got home. I didn't ever tell my friend about it, but from then on, we were careful about snack bowl rules when visiting friends.

Dali worked at the grocery store at the end of our street (Pot Na Polane) in Dragomer. After going to that store several times, she and Dorothy became friendly. In time, she even came to our house for coffee and "pecivo" (cake). Her family situation was that almost all of her immediate family lived in half an apartment in Bosnia. By half an apartment, I don't mean to say that they shared a living space with someone else, I mean that the other half of the apartment was missing, blown up in the war. We talked about what we might be able to do for them, but we didn't have any money.

Dorothy went through all our clothing, including clothes the church had given us. The kids drew pictures to cheer people up, and along with Dorothy's American style sweaters and things, in the end, there were two or three carloads of clothing and some food items such as jam. Dali was so excited it was moving how she carried on about it when we saw her because I had felt a little bad that there wasn't a bunch of money in the gift. Dali came back from Bosnia with a glowing report of how much her family appreciated what we had done. It meant something to the Bosnians that a family they had never met decided to care about them.

For over a year, the prayer group met at our house. At times the house would be so packed, there was barely any sitting room between the living room and kitchen. Other times there were fewer people, but at all times we made good use of the balcony, occasionally grilling "cevapcici" (mixed meat burger rolled into logs), almost always eating pecivo, drinking fruit tea and strong coffee.

One night, three or four of the bums we knew came to the group. It wasn't difficult speaking with them, even though we were 10,000 km from home and only spoke English; Slovenia has the most educated bums I have ever seen. When walking around town, for example, a panhandler once approached me and asked for money in Slovene. I tried to say

"I don´t speak Slovene."

He cut in and said, "O.K., I can speak English, as well as German and a little French, it doesn´t matter." It was incredible that this guy, with the ability to speak four languages was bumming cigarettes and booze money on the street. I was later to learn that as the year gets colder, they move farther and farther south, through Croatia and Bosnia, sometimes to the border of Greece, only to return by the time the weather was warm. They couldn´t get any farther north than the Austrian border.

The night that the bums showed up at our meeting was different from the ordinary homegroup. They were very appreciative of our attention and caring. One even wept out loud and promised to come to the church service sometime. It was weird, though, because these people were utterly raw, having no church experience. I had zero experience with this kind of outreach at home and was unsure of how to manage the prayer meeting. One guy wanted some Band-Aids, even though he had no injury. It turned out that he had his drug stash taped to his leg under his pants. I was immediately uptight and angry. I was upset that anyone would bring something illegal and dangerous into my house where my kids were living. I was worried that something would happen and the police would come. What would happen then? What if they thought I had something to do with the drugs?

Of course, there were no police, and nothing went wrong. Instead we heard Mitija's story about the wife he lost since becoming a bum and all the money he used to have when he ran his own shop. He certainly did not look dangerous. When it was all over, they returned to the city, though precisely where I did not know.

That night, I gave some thought to the difference between that man and me. He had once had a respectable life, complete with a family. If that were true, how did he come to his present condition? I did not know, which meant that I did not know how far I ever was from being in his shoes. Bruce at United Technologies had always said two things, once of which was, "We are all just two bad breaks from the street, we should keep that in mind."

On a different day scheduled for the group in our home, when we were within the hour of starting time, Dorothy began violently throwing up. We didn't know how we could get a hold of people to tell them group was off on account of sickness. We decided to keep Dorothy in the bedroom and hold group as normally as possible. Unfortunately, as group got underway, Dorothy needed to throw up in the bathroom with increasing frequency. That particular day happened to be a near-record attendance day, with people filling the living room and overflowing into the kitchen and hallway in front of the bathroom. After a while, Dorothy was coming out of the bedroom every ten minutes in her bathrobe to barf. The people in the living room probably didn't notice, but it was increasingly uncomfortable for Dorothy. Without trying to describe the echo in our tile bathroom, I can say Dorothy was happy when Daniela arrived because with her came the standard folk knowledge for sickness and remedies. Daniela ordered us to make strong mint tea, letting it steep for fully twelve minutes. Having no mint, she told us to use rosehip instead. Immediately after taking the tea, Dorothy's full-body heaving ceased.

I liked our landlord very much. Matjaz was the assistant professor of mechanical engineering at the university. He said he was qualified to be a professor, but there were not enough openings to go around. One thing I liked about him was that he was the perfect engineering type, very logical and calm, but not unfriendly.

One day, though, he came to me with quite a strange request. I already knew that the house we were renting had been his mother's and that she had passed a few years before. He told me that regularly, their dead mother visited his sister at night. When this happened, she would "suffer very much." She had gone to see one of the very many new age spiritists, who sold her a painting which, according to the spiritist, was painted in particular colors and with such a style that it would bring the spirit of her dead mother to rest. He wanted know if we had a problem with hanging it in each room of the house for a month or so until his sister was released from her "visitations."

I made a quick counter offer. Trying not to offend the man, I carefully explained that we were very much against such things, but would he consider allowing us to pray for his sister, and give God a chance to help her? He seemed a bit relieved and very happy that we were willing to pray for her. We never heard about the picture or her "visitations" again, and they even accepted a couple of Slovene Bibles be kept around the house (The Gideons are everywhere, God bless them!)

Our daughter's friend Petra had a grandmother and grandfather, who were our neighbors. Dorothy often visited over photographs and coffee with probably fifty total words common to them both. She was a very kind and attentive neighbor. When she heard Dorothy coughing across the street, she brought some of her homemade medicine the following day. They were always giving us plums from their yard. Like many, their fruits came from trees and vines that were planted by their grandparents. It was an everyday conversation for neighbors to advise on gardening. He was always calling "sosed" (neighbor) to us from across the street. He was the one who told Dorothy that the stray cat we were going to adopt had been killed by a car: "Tvoja muca je mrtv," that is, "your cat is dead."

After my father's funeral in the United States, Ted decided that he wouldn't go to school anymore; he just flat out refused. Dorothy and I decided to give it a little time and see what would happen if we kept him home for a while. Whereas the school didn't understand, they didn't make trouble.

While I went to work, he and Dorothy planted an expanded the vegetable garden together, while the neighbors helped with plenty of advice. Ted, of course, could translate most of it. Maria would sometimes stand in her yard and call out for Candace to come out and translate, "Candace, pridi sem! After a few weeks, Ted's teacher sent us a package of cards for Ted; every student in his class had made a card, at the direction of the teachers on school time, to ask Ted to please come back because they missed him. When Lubica (Ted's teacher) invited Dorothy to go to class every day so Ted would feel secure, we quickly accepted, feeling that God was making an opportunity for us in relationships. By the end of that year, Dorothy was able to make such a good connection with Lubica, she visited her on occasion outside of the school and was warmly welcomed by Lubica on subsequent visits to Slovenia. Lubica grew to be quite fond of Dorothy; one way we knew this was by her holding hands with Dorothy sometimes when outside the school. It was funny because it´s not the sort of contact casual friends have in the United States, but it is common in Slavic countries, and Dorothy played along anyway, and let the friendship grow.

This was also the class where many field trips are used to supplement the Slovenian kids´ first year of school. We recently tried to count the number of field trips and failed. In one year, the kids saw farms and animals, the city zoo, bomb shelters, a deer preserve, even the mountains on an all-day Saturday trip.

Later in the year, I started an English class for the teachers at the school. Seven or eight teachers participated, most of whom hadn't usually wanted to join any language school classes. They were nervous about lessons, but maybe because they had our kids in school, they felt more comfortable with me. Lubica was in that class too; it was one more way we could get to know ordinary people who were not to be found in the church outreach.

I've heard of school hot lunch programs before, but none I ever saw before or since came close to the experience our kids had in the Log-Dragomer School. The kitchen facility was second to none, with its rows of stainless and chrome ovens and stoves, counters and work areas. It wasn't just for show, either; for about 120 SIT (Slovenian Tolars, for which the exchange rate during our visit slowly rose from 155 SIT per one American dollar to 180 SIT), the kids would get some main course such as wiener schnitzel, soup, potatoes, salad, bread and butter for lunch, with dessert included. For an additional 50 SIT, they would get a "malica" (snack time), which could be anything from Nutella on bread or paté, which Ted loved, and still does. Day to day, the kitchen staff would watch the kids; if they didn't seem to be eating right, they pointed it out to the kids and their parents, if need be. During a parent-teacher day, one of the kitchen staff said, "Your son, Ted, doesn't like rice very much, does he?"

It was just part of the overall attitude there that the school staff constituted a legitimate part of the child's extended family. Wherever I go, there are teachers who care about the children, but in Dragomer, it went beyond that to the extent that some of these teachers were on par with grandparents, aunts, and uncles. Teachers ate with the children and tried to improve their eating habits and manners. The kitchen staff strictly enforced the rule: "You took it, you eat it."

Although the staff served the food as they thought best, the kids could say "Yes" or "No" to it, and could choose additional servings of what they liked. Ted once told us, "You have to pay more when you take more than three helpings." Candace said that her teacher was always hounding her to use a fork for the French fries. More than a year after we moved to Germany, our kids were remembered and warmly greeted with ice cream by the kitchen staff on one of our visits.

At first, whenever we went into the city, we often walked around to get familiar with the layout. We would try the ice cream or "burek" (Balkan meat pie) at different places to see where the best deal was located. After a short time, however, I began to feel that we should return to particular sources for each item or service we wanted. It was obvious from the beginning that "getting in" with the un-churched people of the city would take more time than was afforded to filling a cone with ice cream. If we repeatedly returned to the same place, however, maybe our connection would develop, even if spaced out over time. Although this method is painstaking and requires more time than we spent in Slovenia to make converts, we did see the beginnings of success through relationships. The particular vendors and attendants we patronized did move ahead in conversation, becoming more and more open as we repeatedly returned, ready with a joke or a smile.

When we visited a year after leaving Slovenia, the ice cream man recognized us, and before Dorothy could order, he said "Dve limona, prav?" (two lemon, right?), and the burek man just said, Hey, Michigan." With time, the ladies in the grocery even began helping us with our Slovene, one sentence at a time: "Ali lahko dobim prosim...?" (Could I please get...?).

We were more than a little sobered by what happened to the vegetable man down the road when he disappeared. He was like many others, a foreigner from the South, I think Albania. A very nice guy, who also helped us one word at a time to communicate, he often traveled back and forth between Slovenia and his own country, in spite of the war. Then, one day, he was gone. A different family took over his vegetable "house" at the end of the road. They didn´t know him, and no information was available, he was gone. We had no way of knowing whether he moved on, or if something serious happened to him in the war. We never heard another word about him.

It was certainly different for us to realize people were being killed in a war, no further than a single days' journey by car. Of course, the European standard for distances applies here, where in one day, a person can drive through five countries. Nevertheless, war was not an issue confined to the newspapers. Here, people we knew had families in the middle of it. Later, that would lead to a unique experience for us, as we received letters after we moved to Germany from someone we knew and loved who went back to Serbia and whose entire family endured American bombing. She would often call her mother in Novi Sad from our house in Slovenia to see if her family was still alive. I have no statement about the war, but it was very strange to know someone who was caught in it.

Tony was the butcher in the local grocery store. He was an Amway distributor. When he found out that we were Americans, he nearly went crazy trying to get us to sell for him. The other people in the store even told us about how convinced he was that we would be "able to sell anything" because we were Americans. He was amusing, but also very kind. He was the kind of guy who slipped in extra meat here and there or gave us some prepared dish because he claimed it wouldn't sell before, so he would have to throw it out when we could see he had just made it that same day. He wouldn't come to church, but he was sometimes agreeable to talk a little about "issues." That was typical of Slovenia, that as long as we didn't try to church them right away people would slowly open up and begin sharing hopes, dreams, and disappointments.

We never lost our heart for Slovenia by coming to Germany. Whenever there is a chance to go back, we do everything in our power to get there. When we go, our hearts grow for the people so much that we never regret it. Once, Dorothy visited a cheerleading competition on a visit. So many people recognized her, Brigitte was quite surprised. It made Dorothy cry to hear so many people ask, "When are you coming back?" Not all aspects of all visits proceeded smoothly. When Dorothy and the kids accepted the school's invitation to attend the cheerleading camp on the coast in Piran, Dorothy ran into a reminder of one of the bondages men are under in this country; I suppose the same as many other places.

One of the hosts who worked at the hotel took everyone out on the Adriatic Sea on his boat. After putting out into the middle of the bay, he anchored. Those who wanted to swim jumped in, and those who wanted to lounge stayed put. This man felt free to go around flirting and touching many of the women, trying to be sexy. He went so far as to fondle some of the girls, too. The teachers were angry, but it didn't seem there was much they could do, being women. Dorothy was quite shocked, and when he came her way and tried to put his arm around her waist, she shook her fist in his face and gave him some attitude. He backed off but continued trying to be the playboy with some of the others. The point that dismayed Dorothy was that many of the girls seemed to think nothing of it. Some even made remarks such as: "That's just how it is," or, "A girl should expect men to act like that." I should add that although Christianity has been in the area since ancient times, there is not one evangelical church in the city of Piran. It is also notable, and not surprising that even though Slovenia ranks high in suicide among youth, the rate is even higher in Piran. One person we met even went so far as to say, "I don't know of one single happy family in Piran."

If there is one person who stands for what we are working for, it might be our friend Darja. In time, she did accept Jesus in a service at which Pastor Klingenberg from our home church preached while visiting the Telzerows. The extraordinary factor in our relationship with Darja is that we did not meet her in the church, but through our routine life in the community. When I started teaching classes at a language school down the road from Berlitz, I found that almost all of the teachers were single women, several of whom were quite attractive. As a result, I soon brought Dorothy in for a visit. I learned from my years in the automobile industry that there would be attractive and sexy women I would have to work with, with no escape. My defense was, and is, to ask Dorothy to dress well and pay a few visits to my workplace. By introducing her around, it not only eliminates the feeling that I have a second, secret life, which is the biggest problem, it helps extinguish any secret ideas in the minds of women I know at work. Darja was a teacher of English as well as Slovene and German, so we worked together at times.

When we started an exchange class, in which the teachers agreed to swap language skills on our own time, and Darja was often the only person in my class, I began bringing Dorothy on the pretext that she, too, would like to learn Slovene. Happily, she became friends with Darja herself, and in the end, prepared her to accept Jesus when she came to church with us. Darja and Dorothy went on to become long-term friends.

Street-musicians are a common sight in European cities, so performing is the most natural thing in the world for someone who can sing. Not all singers are Christians, though; in fact, the Hari Krishnas often do street evangelism in Ljubljana, right in the same city square where we did our Christian outreach at different times. They had their electric guitars and keyboards, dancing, singing, smiling girls, and even counselors to guide seekers. There are so many seekers in

Slovenia that these people never seem to fail to bring in a few with every outreach. People, especially youths, are looking for answers, but there are very many different voices trying to provide those answers.

We participated in outreaches to Trbovlje and Kranj, both cities of between twenty and thirty thousand people without a single evangelical church. In Trbovlje, we sang worship songs in the town market, where people were buying their fruits and vegetables. I would naturally have been nervous enough playing music in a church service, but this was something entirely different. In a church, people are expected to play worship music. In a farmer's market, however, there wasn't even special sound arrangements or announcement or anything. I was petrified; to me, this was one wild and crazy experience. As we played, and of course, we sang in Slovene, as usual, many people stopped to listen, and some even laid gifts of fruits and vegetables down for us before leaving. When we were finished, we left. It seems weird to me, but the reality is that the so-called harvest field sits there, day after day, waiting for someone who has the answer to do something. We could go every day to a place like that and give an outreach. It makes a person feel very small and lends meaning to the scripture regarding the harvest being plentiful with few workers.

In Kranj, the outreach was more substantial, including members from another charismatic church in Ljubljana. A generator supplied power for electric guitars and microphones. Rent was paid to the city for permission to sing until about ten at night, and the location was good. There were many interested people who lingered more than an hour after the music was over. As for Dorothy and me, we could not speak Slovene well enough to witness, so we passed out tracts in Slovene. I was surprised at the gratitude some expressed over something so simple as a gospel tract.

One of the many American television shows we occasionally watched in Slovenia was called "Miza Za Pet," or "Party (or table) for Five." It was about a family who struggled to stay together as a family after their parents were killed. The gist of the show for me was that no matter what else happens, the five children, some grown-up, always had each other. I began to call our family "Miza Za Pet" because I meant it. No matter who comes or goes, no matter what criticism people want to dish out, no matter what pressures come our way, the five of us come first, and somewhere around seven billion people come second. It has powerfully proven out that so long as we genuinely stick together in Jesus Christ, we move ahead without fear, and no matter what happens, we stick together.

When we had been in Slovenia for only a short time, the national Pentecostal church invited our kids to attend their church camp, and Dorothy was welcome to come. It was in a region called "Prekmurja," which means "across the Mura (river)." This is on the extreme eastern side of Slovenia, near the Hungarian border. The camp was an experience they will never forget, both good and bad. The facilities were not as comfortable as an American would naturally expect, but more or less adequate. The camp was situated on the top of a mountain ridge, which is not surprising, because, with the exception of one flat area south of Ljubljana, the entire country is covered with low mountains, between 1000 and 2000 feet high.

All in all, the gorgeous area was almost purely agricultural, and the local farmers kept the camp supplied with food. There was so much food that Dorothy reported they were eating up to six times a day. We have a funny saying to describe the Slovenian hospitality, and we mean it warmly, "The Slovenians try to kill you with food."

Wherever we go, food is a necessary part of human interaction. The people there are very active, walking, riding bike, hiking, gardening, etc., such that though they eat very well, they generally are on the slim side more than not. When they meet someone like Dorothy, who often eats very little, they worry about her health and often felt that stuffing her would improve her health.

At the camp, there were three church services per day. The "good morning" service included worship and prayer. Then there was the afternoon activity and Bible service. When it came time for the evening service, though, Dorothy and the kids were in for a bit of a surprise. It seems that after WWII, Slovenia experienced some level of a Holy Spirit revival. While in the city of Novo Mesto (New City), I met a woman who was instrumental in founding the largest charismatic church in Slovenia (150 people); she had seen persecution those post-war days. People lost jobs for being charismatic; insults and rocks were even thrown (this reminds me of our own church's history in Grand Rapids in the early part of the twentieth century, during the birth of the charismatic movement.). I think I'm right in saying that the emerging communist government tolerated the Catholic Church because it was already established, and the communists believed the church would die out. The Pentecostals, however, represented "religious expansion" and was severely frowned upon.

In those days, these Slovenians who were experiencing the power of the Holy Spirit cried out to God with loud, wailing voices, which was followed by God's answer with "holy fire." To this day, therefore, the Pentecostals who live in the areas where the revival started practice this crying out and wailing as a regular part of their worship services. It was such an unexpected and foreign experience that Dorothy was quite unnerved and very uncomfortable. Neither she nor the kids could flow with the service at all. We talked this over many times, especially since I wasn't there; I always have to work, of course. We discuss whether a service like that is different from what we know and so, a matter of cultural adjustment and understanding, or if it is a dead version of something that was once alive and growing. This idea magnifies the very same issue church leaders have tried to deal with at our church back home: "At what point does a move of God become a tradition, and at what point does that same tradition become a ritual?"

It is a very timely question defying a simple answer. I do not make any conclusion regarding the camp in Prekmurja, but it does alter the way I see (and question) the activities of the church in general.

The negative side of the camp was the cold reception Dorothy received because we had joined with Steve Telzerow's church, instead of the Slovenian National Pentecostal Union Church. Contrary to what it sounds like, this is not a government church. It is comparable with the Assembly of God denomination in the United States, except that in this land of two million people, it's estimated five hundred members account for about eighty percent of the total non-Catholic Christians in the country.

In the period immediately before our arrival, the church split up. I cannot comment firsthand on the nature of the church leadership before that point. What I found when I arrived was a situation in which many of the people of that denomination felt they needed a change, but had no other church to choose. These people had complaints about church leadership. There was a group of people, mostly members of the Pentecostal church, who had resigned their memberships and set out to form a separate church. As Steve had been an associate pastor in one of the churches that split into three parts, and as he was an AG missionary pastor from the United States, he was advised by leadership to temporarily back away from formal church duties until the situation could be resolved. Therefore, he neither attended the remains of the former church, nor the new breakaway churches, but maintained personal relationships with the people he knew throughout the week, as before. There was certainly a lot of communication between the officials of the church in Slovenia as well as the United States. Not being a minister, and not being sent by the Assembly of God, I was not privy to those discussions, but neither did I need to be.

It was clear to me from the beginning that my assignment from God was one of encouragement, specifically to Steve and Barbara, the missionary pastors, who happened to be originally from my home church. I received a word from God early on that I was to neither "affirm nor criticize" any of the church structure whatsoever while I was in Slovenia. I was not to comment on anything there that was beyond my scope, which included almost everything there. We were there to lend moral support and emotional encouragement to Steve and Barbara, specifically.

During my initial visit to Slovenia in April 1997, I attended several Pentecostal union services with Steve. When they asked me to speak as a visiting brother from the United States, I did so, testifying to what I had seen and heard in the revival in Grand Rapids. I had opportunity during these visits to meet the leaders of the Pentecostal Union, and I must say they were exceptionally friendly and welcoming to me. For the group of people who were meeting in that house group the night they asked me to perform an anointing service, who became the church we attended, Dorothy and I did our best to fulfill the typical office of Christian and nothing more. Where we could pray, sing, teach, prophecy, or give money, we did so, just like any other member of the body. When some of the people asked me to seek church eldership, however, I declined, not wanting to overstep my boundaries, in light of what God had laid on my heart. In time, we accepted a level of relationship with people from one of the other breakaway churches, but held to the usual role of any member of the body of Christ, seeking to love as many individuals as we could with the love of Jesus. We knew there were some church politics, but we did not involve ourselves in any active way. Wherever we met un-churched people; however, we considered our role to be completely open. Most of the towns in Slovenia do not have a single evangelical church of any kind. Even many Catholic churches are mostly empty, as the people have turned to a wide range of cults and new age groups to fulfill their spiritual needs.

The historic city of Vrnika dates back to the time of the Greek empire, (some people believe that "Jason" from ancient Greek mythology was a real person who died in Vrnika, hence the symbol of the town, an ancient Greek ship). The city has a population of around seventy thousand people but doesn't have a single evangelical church. As far as our friends in the church know, there isn't a single evangelical Christian there.

This sobers me greatly as we pursue the relationship with one of Candace's former schoolteachers who live in Vrnika, who we would never have even met if our kids hadn't insisted on going to school in Slovenia. Many people think either that I am crazy or that I take myself too seriously. I can only say that the thought of making a spiritual difference to people like that schoolteacher is enough to justify giving away everything we had to get there. I do take myself very seriously. If I didn't, I'd still be back in Grand Rapids, assuring Chrysler Corporation that the reliability of their seat adjustment mechanism is good. Many Christians have a valid witness in such a life, but I no longer do. We do not regret coming here, not do we fear the future, regardless of how much or how little money we might make. Our greatest fear is not that we will have no money, rather, that we could fail to continue in relationship with these people through lack of work or money. Somewhere in the world, some people minister to thousands and millions. Once, I thought that to be a great man of God, a person had to have great abilities and do great deeds. Now, I am ready to accept that, if we can only make a difference to at least a handful of people, it will still be worth it. I picture the destruction of the earth coming on, Christians escaping to heaven in their cars, and as if I have a couple of seats empty, and I would like to get some of the people standing around to get in and be saved while they still can. I call this vision, carload on the edge of eternity, and I have made it my life's work from this point forward.

I must state somewhere along the way that I am not a minister of any church denomination. I am not an agent of any foreign missions department, either. That is why I do not call myself a "missionary," though we do missionary work. I do not fit the role that most often comes to mind in the church when that word is used. I want to be careful to avoid even a slight risk that anyone is misled about my qualifications through the misuse of a word. I am aware and am reminded on many occasions in case I should forget that much of the church does not recognize that we are doing anything other than taking a vacation, getting in the way, or "moving around like gypsies." (The fact is, after hearing the plight of the gypsies in a British newsmagazine, I hope to be among them soon, to help.)

A pastor has asked, "how can you fulfill the missionary's role in raising nationals and equipping them for the pastoral ministry, seeing that you have never been a minister and have not been trained yourself according to the five-fold apocalyptic vision?" My answer for us is that I cannot possibly fill this role, so it not our intention at this time. We have come to offer what we have, seeing that our lives probably should have taken a different route much earlier, and that we should have gone off for the standard training when we were young, but that we did not, for whatever reasons. Such as we are, we have a deep desire to reach people who are beyond the current reach of the church. That means working in the mission field, but it doesn't imply working alone, or even independently. It means that we will seek out people who have been raised to be leaders of the church of Jesus Christ, who have become tired or need encouragement. I know from experience now that this is not a fantasy; there are some pastors, foreign missionary national alike, who have a real need for help, encouragement, and prayer. At such time as there is no one who feels he needs more support, I will gladly return home.

Made in the USA
Monee, IL
02 December 2019